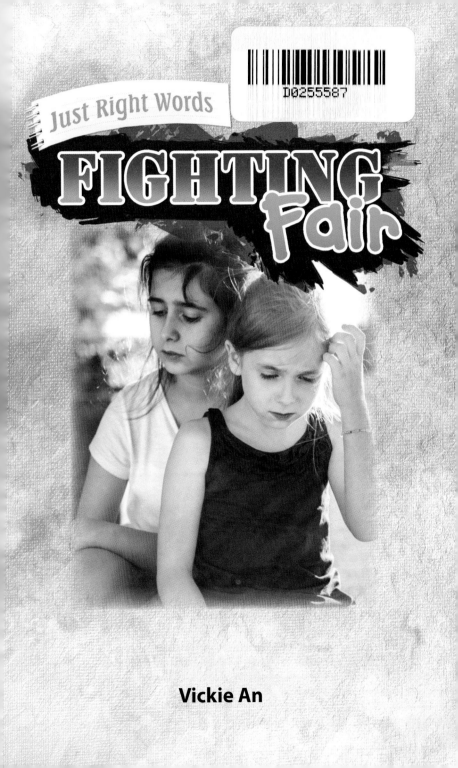

Just Right Words

FIGHTING Fair

Vickie An

Publishing Credits

Rachelle Cracchiolo, M.S.Ed., *Publisher*
Conni Medina, M.A.Ed., *Managing Editor*
Nika Fabienke, Ed.D., *Series Developer*
June Kikuchi, *Content Director*
John Leach, *Assistant Editor*
Lee Aucoin, *Senior Graphic Designer*

TIME For Kids and the TIME For Kids logo are registered trademarks of TIME Inc. Used under license.

Image Credits: p.10 dpa picture alliance/Alamy Stock Photo; p.13 Cultura RM/Alamy Stock Photo; p.16 Jessica Antola/Contour by Getty Images; p.20 Dinodia Photos/Getty Images; p.21 Meibion/Alamy Stock Photo; p.23 (top left) National Archives [1667751], (top right) National Archives [1408042], (bottom) Library of Congress [LC-USZC4-9904]; p.25 Bas Czerwinski/AFP/Getty Images; all other images from iStock and/or Shutterstock.

Teacher Created Materials
5301 Oceanus Drive
Huntington Beach, CA 92649-1030
http://www.tcmpub.com
ISBN 978-1-4258-4975-7
© 2018 Teacher Created Materials, Inc.

Table of Contents

What Is Fair?

What is your favorite game at recess? Jeremy's favorite is basketball. When the bell rings, he races outside to scoop up a ball before they are all taken. But today, Jeremy and Noah both grab the last basketball at the same time.

"I was here first," Jeremy says.

"No, *I* was!" Noah replies. He **wrestles** the ball away and runs toward the court. "You're too slow!"

"That's not fair!" Jeremy shouts.

Responding the Right Way

Have you ever thought you were being treated unfairly? Sometimes these feelings bubble up when we disagree or when we do not get our way. But how we react to conflicts can make a difference in working them out. Most of all, it is important to fight fair.

Defining "Fair"

Fairness can mean a number of things. It can mean playing by the rules or treating others the way you want to be treated. It can mean sharing or giving everyone the same chance. Fighting fair is when you solve a problem with kindness and respect.

Share Your Feelings

When we disagree with others, bad feelings are sure to follow. It is normal to feel hurt or angry. It is also important to understand why. What do you feel is unfair? Think about what is bothering you. Then share your feelings.

Ground Rules for Fighting Fair

Follow these rules for a fair discussion. First, you must stay calm. Are you feeling worked up? Take some deep breaths, close your eyes, and count backward from 10. By calming your mind, you can stop yourself from saying things you will **regret** or cannot take back.

Get Your Anger Out

It's not wise to bottle up your anger. You might explode! When you are upset, you may feel like yelling, hitting, or breaking things. Instead, do some jumping jacks or run around to release some negative energy. Or shake off the anger by dancing!

Grab a Pen

Sometimes, writing down your feelings can help release anger. What made you mad? Write a list of everything that upset you, and do not stop until you are calm. Or draw your feelings instead.

Are you ready to have a calm discussion? That's great! Here is another tip to keep in mind. When explaining why you are upset, try to use words such as "I feel ____ when you ____ because ____." And remember, being honest is always best. So be as truthful as you can with the other person.

At the same time, do not be hurtful. You should not put others down or call them names. Do not yell or put your hands on them. Do not use excuses, and do not **accuse** people. Doing these things will only add to the problem. Being aggressive or mean will not help.

What will happen when Jeremy and Noah follow these ground rules for fighting fair? Let's find out.

You, You, You!

"*You* make me angry!" "*You* are wrong!" "*You* are a bad friend!" Using the word "you" like this can lead to hurt feelings. It is tempting to blame others during an argument. But pointing fingers will do more harm than good.

"I Feel"

Using the words "I feel" can help you express your feelings. These words do not blame or accuse the other person. They can help get your message across in a more polite and kind way.

Jeremy informs their teacher, Ms. Lee, about what happened. They walk over to the field, and Ms. Lee calls Noah over. The boys plop down on the grass.

"Jeremy, please tell Noah why you are upset," Ms. Lee says.

Jeremy takes a deep breath. "Noah," he says, "I felt mad when you grabbed the basketball because I wanted to play. I also felt bad when you said I was too slow."

Jeremy has **expressed** his feelings. Then, Noah shares that he is also bothered because he never gets to play basketball at recess. Where should they go from here?

The Power of Words

Langston Hughes (LANG-stun HYOOZ) was a famous poet and writer. During his life, black people did not have the same rights as white people. He used his words to share his hope that one day all people would be equal.

Writing the Blues

Langston Hughes often wrote poetry in the style of blues music. Blues songs describe trouble or sadness but many times in a funny way. What are some things that give you the blues? Too much homework? Arguing with your best friend?

Same Ground Rules at Home

Do you have siblings? If you do, then you have probably fought with them. Maybe everyone wants the last cookie. Or maybe you all want to use the computer at the same time. You will not get along all the time. Use the skills you just learned to solve problems with family, too.

When brothers or sisters **compete**, it is called sibling rivalry. This is not always a bad thing. Sometimes it can make you work harder.

For example, maybe your brother runs faster than you. This might make you want to practice more so you can become better. But sometimes too much competition can cause problems. You might feel so upset that you say something hurtful.

Family Size

Family size is different around the world. In the United States, an **average** family has two children. In some parts of Asia, families have one child on average. That is not the case in Niger (NIE-jer) in Africa. There, families have about seven kids on average.

Siblings and Sports

Most siblings compete with each other. Even famous siblings compete! Venus and Serena Williams are top tennis stars. Peyton and Eli Manning rule the football field. Pau and Marc Gasol are basketball champs. These siblings play against each other. They cheer for each other, too.

Think of Solutions

There is more than one side to every fight. Fighting fair means listening to the other person. Showing **empathy** is important. It helps you see the problem in a new way.

Practice Empathy

Here is how you can practice showing empathy. First, listen closely to the other person. Then, think of how you would feel if the same thing happened to you. Ask the other person how he or she feels. Finally, show you care by asking how you can help or by offering a hug.

Put Yourself in Their Shoes

Do you know what it means to "put yourself in someone else's shoes"? Here is an example. Your friend is sad because her cat ran away. How would you feel if that happened to you? If you answered "sad," you understand how she feels. That is empathy.

Practice Active Listening

Use **active listening** skills to show you are paying attention. Nod to show you understand. Ask questions. Then, restate what the person said. Tell the speaker you understand how he or she feels.

Say Sorry

It can be hard to apologize. Saying it directly is the most important way. People around the world show that they are sorry in different ways. Giving gifts is one way to apologize. In the United States, a common gift that says "I'm sorry" is flowers. People in Korea like to give apples. Why? The Korean word for apple is also the word for apology.

Saying sorry is just one step. After everyone gets a chance to talk, think about what was said. What part did you play in the fight? What would you change? Learn from your mistakes. Then, work on a solution together.

Lessons for All

"On the Pulse of the Morning" is a poem by Maya Angelou (MYE-uh AN-juh-loo). She wrote it for the **inauguration** of President Bill Clinton in 1993. The poem asks us to learn from the past. That way, we will not make the same mistakes in the future.

Fix the Problem

Now it is time to fix the problem. Finding an answer that everyone likes is not always easy. Make sure to listen to everyone's thoughts. It might help to go over the **advantages** and **disadvantages** of an idea.

You will not always agree. But try to be a good sport. You can do so in a few ways. Be polite. Treat others with respect. Accept your part in the disagreement. And be kind when the argument is over.

Brainstorming Tips

Remember that the point of **brainstorming** is to come up with a lot of ideas, even if you do not use them all. Think about your goal. What problem do you want to solve? Jot down your thoughts on a piece of paper to stay organized.

Take a Stand

Many people have fought to make the world a better place. Sometimes, a community feels that something is unfair. Its members will act to change things. They work together. This way, their voices will be heard.

There are a lot of ways groups can peacefully show their feelings. They may set up a **protest** to support their cause. They might organize a boycott. This is when people refuse to buy, use, or take part in something as part of a protest. Or they might start a petition. A petition is a written request for change. Supporters sign it. Then they give it to someone in power.

Peace from India

Mohandas Gandhi (MOH-hahn-duhs GAHN-dee) fought against the unfair treatment of his people. He used peaceful **methods**. He once led a march for 241 miles (388 kilometers) to protest an unfair law.

RISE UP FOR THE CLIMATE
YES TO SOLAR

friends of
the earth
see things differently

RISE UP FOR THE CLIMATE
YES TO SOLAR

friends of
the earth
see things differently

Test It Out

A compromise (KAHM-pruh-myz) is when each person gives up something to reach an agreement. You are not always going to get your way. But if you work together, everyone can be happy. So, brainstorm first. Then, pick a solution that you both like, and test it out.

In Jeremy and Noah's case, each boy gave up having the basketball all to himself during recess. They decided to compromise by taking turns. But soon another problem came up. They both wanted to be the first to play. *Uh-oh!* How will they solve this one?

Let's Make a Deal

"You scratch my back, and I'll scratch yours!" Have you heard anyone say this? It is all about compromising to reach a common goal. It reminds us that if each side can give a little bit, then everyone will get some of what they want.

Did You Know?

Even people who help build nations have to compromise. The Founding Fathers created the U.S. Constitution in 1787. But they had to come up with a plan that would make each state happy. The final document is a set of rules for the government.

Coming to an agreement is just part of working through a problem. Sometimes when you put an idea into action, it might not work. When that happens, do not give up. Go back to the drawing board, and choose another idea. Or come up with new ones, and test them out. Keep trying until you find a solution that works.

It can be disappointing when an idea that you try doesn't work. You will not always succeed the first time. But **persevere**!

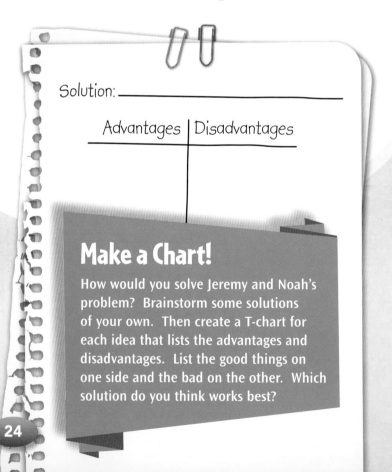

Solution: _____

Advantages	Disadvantages

Make a Chart!

How would you solve Jeremy and Noah's problem? Brainstorm some solutions of your own. Then create a T-chart for each idea that lists the advantages and disadvantages. List the good things on one side and the bad on the other. Which solution do you think works best?

Never Give Up

Malala Yousafzai (mah-LAH-lah yoo-sahf-ZAY) inspires many kids. She grew up in Pakistan. She spoke out about girls' right to education. She was attacked for her beliefs. But she survived. She continues to fight for schooling for all.

Problem Solved!

Jeremy and Noah list ways to solve their problem, but they cannot seem to agree. Suddenly, something shiny catches Jeremy's eye. It's a quarter. Jeremy suggests that they flip the coin to see who will shoot the basketball first. Noah agrees and asks Ms. Lee to be the referee. She flips the quarter. Noah calls tails. And it is heads! The boys accept the outcome and walk to the basketball court together.

It took time, but Jeremy and Noah solved their problem by fighting fair. They used words to communicate their feelings, and they listened to one another. They brainstormed and compromised. And the best part? They both get to play basketball.

Did You Know?

In basketball, a jump ball determines who gets the ball first. One player from each team comes to the center of the court. The referee tosses the ball into the air. The players try to tip the ball over to their side.

Heads or Tails

In football, coin tosses are used to decide who gets to kick off first. One team's captain will call heads or tails. If he calls correctly, he chooses which team will kick off.

Glossary

accuse—to place blame on someone

active listening—paying attention to what someone is saying

advantages—something helpful; pros

average—the usual in a group; being ordinary

brainstorming—spending time to think about ideas or solutions

compete—to work very hard for something, such as a prize, for which someone else is also working very hard

disadvantages—something not helpful; cons

empathy—an understanding of others' feelings

expressed—made known using words

inauguration—a ceremony to put someone into office

methods—plans for doing something

persevere—to do something even if it is hard

protest—an event where people gather to show that they do not approve of something

regret—to be sorry for

wrestles—strongly pulls

Index

Check It Out!

Books

Dr. Seuss. 1971. *The Lorax*. Random House Books for Young Readers.

Schmidt, Fran, and Alice Friedman. 1989. *Fighting Fair for Families*. Peace Education Foundation.

Sornson, Bob. 2013. *Stand in My Shoes: Kids Learning About Empathy*. Love and Logic Press.

Videos

Clinton Presidential Library. *Maya Angelou's Poem "On the Pulse of Morning."* White House Television Crew. www.youtube.com/watch?v=59xGmHzxtZ4.

Websites

U.S. Department of State. *Active Listening*. www.state.gov/m/a/os/65759.htm.

Kids Helpline. *Handling Family Fights*. www.kidshelpline.com.au.

Thirteen.org. *Communication Skill Building*. www.thirteen.org/peaceful/strate.html.

Try It!

You have just learned rules for fighting fair. Use your new skills to help settle these fictional problems. On a piece of paper, brainstorm three different solutions to each. Explain what you would do or say.

- Your class is outside at recess. Lucas and Jorge are racing. Both boys zoom across the finish line. It is a close one! They start to argue over who won. How would you help Lucas and Jorge solve this disagreement?

- Today's art project is to paint your favorite place. Zoe and Katie sit at the same table. They both want to use the blue paint. Zoe complains that Katie is using up all of the blue paint. How will you help Zoe and Katie come to a compromise?

About the Author

Vickie An was born and raised in Houston, Texas, and graduated with a journalism degree from the University of Texas at Austin. She has worked and lived in countries all over the world, including Papua New Guinea and South Korea. Before moving overseas, she lived in New York City and worked as a writer and editor for *TIME FOR KIDS*. Along with her husband, Chris, she enjoys traveling, experiencing different cultures, and trying new foods.